Charismatic Destiny III
Bible Study Curriculum

JANUARY   **SHAKEN NOT STIRRED**
          A. FEAR & PERCEPTION
          B. FAITH ACTIVATION
          C. MIRACLES, SIGNS AND WONDERS
          D. DEMONSTRATIONS

FEBRUARY   **RECKLESS LOVE**
          A. GOSPEL OF GRACE
          B. GOSPEL OF WORKS
          C. GOSPEL AFTER SALVATION
          D. GOSPEL OF DELIVERANCE

MARCH   **SERVANT LEADERSHIP**
          A. YOU'RE UNDER ARREST
          B. ESTABLISHING YOUR GOINGS
          C. COVERING
          D. ADDRESSING ISSUES
          E. THE NEED IS THE CALL

APRIL   **TAKING THE LEAD**
          A. POSITION
          B. PERMISSION
          C. PRODUCTION
          D. DEVELOPMENT

MAY   **FAMILY ROLES AND RESPONSIBILITIES**
          A. FATHER
          B. MOTHER
          C. CHILDREN
          D. FAMILY

JUNE   **THRONE OCCUPATION**
          A. WHO ARE YOU
          B. WHO HAVE THEY MADE YOU
          C. WHO HE SAYS YOU ARE
          D. WHO IS HE
          E. WHERE ARE YOU

JULY **CONNECTED**
- A. NOUNS
- B. MANIFESTATION
- C. GODLY/UNGODLY
- D. FREEDOM

AUGUST **CAN YOU SEE IT...**
- A. GLORY
- B. WIND
- C. RAIN
- D. FIRE

SEPTEMBER **JESUS, BE A FENCE**
- A. HEALTHY BOUNDARIES
- B. SAY NO!!!
- C. BONDAGE OF A YES
- D. BUILD A BRIDGE
- E. PERMISSION GRANTED

OCTOBER **COLLECT $200**
- A. FINDING BALANCE
- B. GOOD STEWARD
- C. SOWING
- D. REAPING

NOVEMBER **DO YOU HEAR WHAT I HEAR**
- A. PROPHECY
- B. THE WRITTEN WORD
- C. MEDIA (TV, RADIO & MUSIC)
- D. JOURNALING

DECEMBER **GIFTS OF THE SPIRIT**
- A. DISCERNMENT OF SPIRITS
- B. TONGUES AND INTERPRETATION
- C. GIFTS OF HEALING
- D. WORKING OF MIRACLES
- E. OPERATING IN LOVE

FEAR & PERCEPTION

a. Fear vs. Love
b. Grappling with Fear
c. Cast it out & Use your love
d. *ACTIVATION – Pray – Break into groups and expose the fears that has kept you in bondage.

PRINCIPLE: Fear can paralyze you, but is overcome, every time with Love

ASK YOURSELF: What was I afraid of last year, that kept me from moving forward?

MEMORY VERSE: 1 John 4:18 – There is no fear in Love; but perfect love casteth out fear: because fear hath torment. He that feareth is now made perfect in love.

REAL LIFE: Sometimes prayer seems useless...how do I deal with this?

In evaluating fear, you often feel like the thing that you fear is justified. There is a root somewhere in your heart surrounding the thing that you fear so you think that the fear you have is valid. If you fear dogs, it is often attributed to an experience that you have had. Understanding that experiences don't go away without addressing the thing that initiated the deposit of fear. In order to deal with the fear, you have to be open to experiencing healing in that area. The way that healing comes is through love. God's love is perfect, and it perfects those things within each of us. Even the places that once caused fear are removed through the Father's perfect love for us when we trust and allow Him to do it for us.

Understanding that fear limits your ability to grow, what are some things that have caused fear for you that has prevented growth for you? What do you believe are ways that you can overcome these fears? Fear paralyzes your ability to grow and prosper and that prevents your ability to get to where God is calling you. Open your heart to the ability of being free and allow Gods' love to perfect you and cause fear to leave.

Pray and ask God to show you the areas where fear has held you captive. As He shows you the areas of fear in your heart, pray that fear in that area be removed and that God replaces it with His perfect love. Remember that fear doesn't exist within love and that means that once His pure love is present fear must flee.

FAITH ACTIVATION

a.   The word is our Anchor
b.   How do you get to know God?
c.   If you want to prophesy, preach or perform miracles, get into His word
d.   The principles of scripture work for EVERYONE, not just believers.
e.   ***ACTIVATION…" What are some principles that work for everyone…what scripture?

PRINCIPLE: Realize that the word is the foundation of the life of the believer. It is the anchor to the ship that is your relationship with God.

ASK YOURSELF: Are all of my spiritual experiences based in the word of God?

MEMORY VERSE: Matthew 24:35 – Heaven and earth shall pass away, but my words shall not pass away.

REAL LIFE: If you do not know the word, nothing else is going to sustain you.

Often the experiences that we face have the ability to overtake us because we don't know what we possess based on the promises of God. The word is the foundation of who we are and in order to know what you possess and are entitled to you must first know the word. In order for you to know your family or friends you have to spend time with them. Spending time in the word causes there to be an understanding of who you were created to be and what the promises are concerning your life. The word is solid and sure. Things and circumstances can change but the word remains. When things begin to happen to you and around you it helps to know what you have in your arsenal to use to help you. As you evolve you need to be able to understand that the word of God sustains you and keeps you and without your commitment and focus to study the word you then negate some of the promises because you don't even know what they are. Get in your word so that you solid and held together by your anchor.

Being active in your word also allows you to get to know God more. Reading your word is one of the ways that you can get to know him. You can also get to know Him through prayer and time alone with Him. In order to understand and know what His thoughts are toward you, time has to be spent in your word and spending time with the Father. You can't make time for everything else and then think that you will give God the sloppy seconds that you have left over. You can't have everything in your life being more important than you finding out who God is for you and what He requires from you. We often think that we can live based of the word that is given to us by others. However fresh revelation for you and your situation is what happens when you get to know the word and God for yourself. If you want to see miracles, signs and wonders you must live in the word and by the word. You miss that when you are only using what you have heard from others. You don't have your own experience or understanding you are going off the experiences of others.

In order to minister and live according to what the word describes you have to get into your word and study to show yourself approved. Don't limit your experience in getting to know the word and God by living through the experiences of others.

MIRACLES, SIGNS AND WONDERS

a. Fasting is necessary to humble yourself.
b. Fasting is not an option, suggestion or idea, it is expected
c. The different kinds of fast will produce different results in you.
d. ***ACTIVATION...Select your fast days and what kind of fast you're going to do.

PRINCIPLE: Fasting speaks to your appetite and yourself control not just not eating.

ASK YOURSELF: What is the effectiveness of fasting?

MEMORY VERSE: Matthew 6:16-18

REAL LIFE: If there is no sacrifice, your expectations for miracles, signs and wonders are for naught.

One of the things that you must understand is that the sacrificing of fasting causes a response from God. Fasting decreases the flesh nature which is our sin nature. This causes our ability to be closer to the heart of God because we have decreased our flesh. Humility comes with our fasting and it is because we have had the ability to deny our flesh and allow the sensitivity of our spirit to connect to the heart of God. Fasting can seem complex and difficult as your flesh desires what it wants when it wants it. Without restriction it knows no boundaries but also feels in control to demand whatever it wants. There are things that you will face that require your flesh to be subject to the Holy Spirit and not in control of you. We see all through scripture how the response to sacrifice was different than the demand or request with no sacrifice. We also see in scripture that faith without works is dead. This confirms that in everything there is a requirement for us to do something. You want to see the manifestation of miracles in your life or the life of your family. Then start sacrificing, not just your food but your time and attention.

In order to accomplish that which our Father has promised we will have to do what is required. There are different types of fast and depending on what you need and what sacrifice He is asking for should determine how you decide to fast. Fasting enhances our fellowship with the Father, cleanses our temple and gives us guidance. Absolute fast would be where you eat nothing. Supernatural Fast would be more reflective of Moses and Jesus fasting for 40 days. Then there is a partial/token/denial which varies in time, length and the what you sacrifice. The partial/denial fast is one that is very common and often used for discipline and answers. Although there are different types of fast each one causes there to be something different that happens within you and to the things that are concerning you. In Duet. 9:9 and Luke 4:2 we see how Moses and Jesus fasted for 40 days. In Acts 9:9 we see how Paul fasted. We see the fruit of fasting which shows us why the principle is necessary.

Evaluate the last thing that you struggled with. Did you fast and seek God for resolve? If so, did that cause you to fast for more things? If you haven't fasted I challenge you to fast over the next two weeks and watch God move!

DEMONSTRATIONS

a) Foot washing, communion, and water baptism
b) Meaning & Belief regarding them
c) Not a Heaven and Hell issue

ACTIVATION – Foot washing and communion

PRINCIPLE: The ordinances of the church are practiced by the church, because we believe, not in order to believe.

ASK YOURSELF: Do I really know the whole meaning behind all of the ordinances? Is my faith elevated because of my participation?

MEMORY VERSE: Psalms 85:2

REAL LIFE: The ordinances of the church that one may take part in doesn't speak to their ability to enter into heaven, but it does speak to humility and the desire of servanthood.

The ordinances of the church aren't required to enter heaven but they are symbolic of our faith and what we believe. Foot washing being one that Jesus implemented Himself, shows us that even the greatest leader of all had to have a servants heart. When Jesus washed the feet of the disciples it showed that even a leader can serve. This also showed humility. That as a leader he wasn't too big to serve those that served with Him. It takes a great leader to be able to show those that they lead that their leader isn't beyond or above serving.

Communion is another ordinance in our church. Communion being a symbol of remembrance of the ultimate sacrifice that was made for us. This ordinance allows for us to show honor in a demonstration of recognition for what was given in order for us to have the right to be free. This is an ordinance that you can do as often as you remember the sacrifice that was made for you.

Water baptism is one of the ordinances of the church that is often debated across denominations. Some believe it to be a requirement and others believe it to be a choice. Regardless of where you fall baptism is still idolized as a symbol of commitment, renewal and being born again for some. Jesus was water baptized along with many others. So just like every other ordinance in the church you can choose to participate and honor what the ordinance represents or, you can choose to not participate for your own varying reasons. But evaluate your why for any ordinance and make sure it is done with a pure heart.

Although these ordinances don't determine heaven or hell. You should study to gain an understanding so that whatever ordinances you choose to follow that your heart is in them and that you are not just doing them to follow the pattern of others.

a) Is there a such thing as too much grace preaching?
b) What is the gospel of grace?
c) As a believer what does grace do for me?

ACTIVATION – Name things that you have been working for that belong to you already?

PRINCIPLE: By grace are you saved!!!

ASK YOURSELF: Are you working for something that has been given to you for free?

MEMORY VERSE: Ephesians 2:8 – For by grace are ye saved, through faith; and that not of yourselves: it is the gift of God.

REAL LIFE: What have I been taught as it pertains to me, making it to heaven.

When it comes down to knowing about your salvation, it is more important to understand what the bible says above all else. Understanding the heart of God as it pertains to salvation and what grace is, is necessary for understanding your place of salvation. Grace has several different definitions. Two of the ones that we are going to use is courteous goodwill and the free will and unmerited (unearned) favor (approval, act of kindness beyond what is due).

The bible says that we are saved because of the act of kindness that goes beyond what is due to us, by His favor and we receive this by what is not seen. Our salvation is a gift of love. Have you ever been angry at someone you loved and because of your love for them, when you grabbed a bag of chips, you got one for them? It's not that they deserved it, nor did you really want to do it, but because of your love for them, an action was done. Whatever they did to upset you was done, they never repented for it, they haven't asked for forgiveness neither have they apologized, but the service is still done.

We can celebrate the fact that there has never been anything good enough that we could do in order to meet the requirements of being good enough. Our righteousness is literally as good as a menstruation pad...nobody in their right mind wants to keep that. As good as we think we are or could have been, it would never have been good enough and because He loves us, he has chosen to extend to us courteous good will; He is giving to us salvation, because he knows that we cannot earn it, buy it or work for it. Celebrate the fact that in order to receive this great gift, all we have to do is confess with our mouths and believe in our hearts that God has raised Jesus from the dead, and our names are written in the Lambs book of life. Is there growth that's necessary? Is there sanctification that needs to happen? Are there things that need to be developed and groomed in us? Absolutely!!! We are talking about his Great grace, not all that other stuff...yet.

GOSPEL OF WORKS

a) What acts of faith are necessary in order to receive the gospel?
b) What do I need to do to be receive the gospel?
c) When preaching the gospel, what am I telling people?

ACTIVATION – What are some things you thought were necessary in order to get saved?

PRINCIPLE: Salvation has nothing to do with what you can do, but with everything Christ has done.

ASK YOURSELF: Is my salvation based on what I can do and keep right, or on what Christ has already done?

MEMORY VERSE: Romans 3:24 – Being justified freely by his grace through the redemption that is in Christ Jesus.

REAL LIFE: We have been taught that salvation comes through us stopping things that we are doing, truth is that we need salvation in order to stop some of the things that we are doing.

It is wonderful to sit and watch the people go to church, help people, dress appropriately, as well as give and help in their church and community. These believers would never willfully commit a crime, commit adultery or steal. The only issue that we could see with them is that they are constantly looking into the lives of other people and telling people everything they are doing wrong and how badly they need to go to church and live for God. I know somebody is going to say that we are supposed to provoke each other to good works, we are, while at the same time dealing with our own hearts. In Matthew 23, Jesus gives a whole teaching about these kinds of people. He said not to be like a certain group of people and equated their teachings to yeast in bread. It spreads easily and quickly and causes everything to expand. As long as you meet these particular requirements, then you will be fine as you, do what we are telling you to do, you'll make it in.

The group were the Pharisees, and they were hypocrites. They put on an act. Not just that they weren't doing things right, but you never did it right. If there was something that you struggled with, it was the worst thing in the world. They held people to a place of holiness that they have declared without realizing that they themselves could not sustain. They were quick to pass judgement on other people and slow to extend mercy...they were the ones that would quickly turn their noses up at the saints who had obvious issues of struggle (smoking, drinking, the things you could see or smell), but Jesus said that they were like graves full of dead men's bones.

They maintained the law and wanted to make sure that everyone else followed it to. Here is the issue, in 2 Corinthians 3:6, the bible let's us know that we have been made good enough as ministers, under the new covenant, not of the letter of the law because the letter kills and the spirit gives life. Using the word to control or destroy someone is never the intent of the book. Be baptized, speak in tongues, quit that smoking, come to church...All of these things need to be done, but they are not essential for salvation. We work because we have been given grace to salvation, not in order to get it.

GOSPEL AFTER SALVATION

a) Justified by faith, but what's the good news after I'm saved?
b) Is life going to change after salvation?
c) What good after salvation?

ACTIVATION – Name some things that God has spoken over your life!!!

PRINCIPLE: There is good news after salvation, for every believer.

ASK YOURSELF: Am I making sure that I am taking advantage of all that God has declared to me?

MEMORY VERSE: 2 Peter 1:3 – According as his divine power hath given unto us all things that pertain unto life and godliness, through the knowledge of him that hath called us to glory and virtue.

REAL LIFE: Going to church and believing is not all that there is to being a believer.

If salvation speaks to us being rescued and the gospel is good news, I'm here to tell you that there is good news after you have been rescued. It is typical for a person to come to the knowledge of Jesus Christ, receive him in their hearts and start walking in the kingdom and then all of a sudden life hits and boom, they forget about their covenant and the fact that God has promised them some things after salvation. We have been given several promises regarding what God would do in and through us.

According to God's divine power, he has already given us everything that is specific for life....and godliness. This is the gospel after salvation. He's placed everything we need in us, around us, or right in our grasp in order to show forth His glory in excellence. After salvation, He rescues us with His word. The promises of God are all written in scripture. He is the reason that we can get wealth. He put his word above his name, his word holds the worlds together, so I know that he will honor what He has said.

The Holy Spirit is a tool that we can use. He is a gift to us to use in the times when we need to learn and understand anything. It is the Holy Spirit that brings all that God has said back from the crevices of our spirits into reality. He has given us the gifts of the Holy Spirit. From faith, to tongues, to the interpretation of those tongues, he has positioned us to be able to do, supernaturally, what we could not do on our own.

Finally, He desires that we would be in health, as our souls prosper. It is his goal to cause all things to work for our good. Life is going to keep going. It will rain some days when you want the sun to shine. It will snow badly on days that you expected it to be nice and breezy. There will be disappointments and times when things just don't work out, the benefit of all of it, is that it will work out for your good and above that, He will never leave you. You will never be by yourself.

GOSPEL OF DELIVERANCE

a) The gospel = good news + Deliverance = continued freedom in Jesus
b) Deliverance isn't just about demons
c) Continued growth and submission to God will cause the devil to flee
d) True freedom is seen in a changed mind and behavior.

ACTIVATION – Focus on Mindsets – What mindsets do you feel like you have got to change. (We can cast out demons later)

PRINCIPLE: The good news of Jesus, allows us to be free from demonic attack, mental anguish and cycles.

ASK YOURSELF: How do I transform my mind set?

MEMORY VERSE: Romans 12:2 – And be not conformed to this world: but be ye transformed by the renewing of your mind, that ye may prove what is that good, and acceptable, and perfect will of God.

REAL LIFE: The good news is that God sets us free from bondages, the bad news is that we have to walk the process out.

There is a wonderful book out called "Crazy Faith". The writer describes in great detail, regarding the act of deliverance (casting out demons) as well as the responsibility of the believer to maintain wholeness by "doing their work". This means that we have to do what is necessary in order to keep our house clean. The memory verse talks about not being conformed, or squeeze into the image or behavior of the world but be able to switch it up, by renewing or renovating your mind. There are steps to renovation, planning, demolition, HVAC, Electrical and plumbing, framing and painting and then adding fixtures. You don't just go in and start tearing stuff down and then throw in a table.

As believers it is our responsibility to renovate our minds. The liberty of deliverance is the fact that you are no longer in bondage or controlled by what your mind tells you, but by the Spirit of God and His word. We talk about deliverance being about casting out demons, but that's just the beginning. As we continue our growth and development in the kingdom, we have to realize that even after the demon is gone, the bible shows us that it is our job to keep our house swept and clean.

Your house needs to be cleaned from top to bottom. How many of you have ever cleaned your house one time and stopped? Your house needs to be cleaned daily, so why would your house, your temple only needs to be cleaned by going to one seminar. Every opportunity to clean your house should be taken. Picking up little papers, washing the dishes, sweeping the floor, rearranging the room, all of those things are necessary. How, you may ask? Well, using the water of the word, worship and repentance, communion with God, worship and fellowship with the saints, forgiveness are tools we can use in order to keep our house clean. Like Captain Planet used to say: The power is yours!!!

YOU'RE UNDER ARREST

a) Limited authority, is still authority
b) Recognizing my boundaries in leadership
c) Servitude isn't slavery...or is it?
d) What is my position in active leadership?

ACTIVATION – Identify your scope of leadership, where should you be leading and what is your responsibility.

PRINCIPLE: We can always point out the negatives about good and bad leaders, but what did you learn?

ASK YOURSELF: What is my responsibility in leadership and to whomever I have submitted to?

MEMORY VERSE: Matthew 8:9 – For I am a man under authority, having soldiers under me: and I say to this man, Go, and he goeth; and to another, Come and he cometh; and to my servant, Do this, and he doesth it.

REAL LIFE: Realize that our individual authority has limits and we have to recognize that even though we have authority we have to make sure we are submitted as well.

Every person in this world has someone that they are submitted to. Have you allowed yourself to be one set under authority so that you can understand your true authority? No man in this world answers to no one. Even the CEO of the company you would for has to answer to his board of directors. The POTUS, answers to congress. No matter how high in position we go, we have to be able to submit to someone.

Did you know that it is absolutely legal to make a citizen's arrest? You have the ability to see a thief and stop them and hold them until the police get's there. Did you catch that? You have the authority to do it until the police get's there. Working with a leader should cause you to see that you are a forerunner. David had Jonathan, Jesus had you and your pastor has you. The person who makes a citizens arrest does a good job. They have stopped the escalation of prices for the average person, maintained the safety of everyone in the store as well as stopped a criminal. It is basically your responsibility to take care of what you have been assigned to.

The story in Matthew speaks to someone that has a heart for the people that are under them. He went out of his way to make sure that his servant was taken care of and healed. He identified his position as well as the servant that was under him, and identified Jesus' authority. It pays to make sure to make sure you recognize who you are, who's around you as well as where your authority comes from.

ESTABLISHING YOUR GOINGS

a) Do you know where you are, why you are there, and where you are going?
b) Have you committed to the vision?
c) What did God say?
d) What is the vision of your local ministry, your life, your ministry?

ACTIVATION – Vision boards for life!

PRINCIPLE: Your commitment to your local ministry impacts your personal vision.

ASK YOURSELF: Can you commit to somebody else's vision in order to see yours?

MEMORY VERSE: Psalms 40:2 – He brought me up out of a horrible pit, out of the miry clay, and set me feet upon a rock, and established my goings.

REAL LIFE: Sometimes God puts you in a place to learn what to do and what not to do, no matter what, honor your commitment!!!

Have you ever been in a position where you have been left in charge because whoever is the boss or the senior leader had to do something else? It is in these times that it becomes extremely important you should know the vision of the leader. The bible tells us without a vision the people perish. That word used in the Hebrew is boundaries. Without boundaries the people will end up in destruction. If you are a part of an organization, a business, ministry or family you have a vision for it. Before you got together you wanted to do this white picket fence with 2.5 children and a dog. That's a vision and the boundaries you should have set should have been in saving for the house, picking the right person etc. The same goes for the business.

I worked for a knife company, and two vacuum companies. The pricing for the vacuums were over the thousand mark. I was able to sale them, because I believed in the vision of the company and the product. As you go forward in ministry your actions should reflect the fact that you believe in the vision of your local church (as long as it aligns with the word of God). If you are looking to do ministry, be active in your local ministry and build it. Trust me, you will reap what you sow. If you are lackadaisical in your effort in supporting another man's ministry, you will reap that in yours. Even if that goal is family or business. While you were apart of another persons company, put your best effort in so that you will reap that in your employees.

There are times when you feel as if the person in charge is not good enough or smart enough to do the job, and that you could do the job better, and you probably could. If you are there, it is probably God's plan for you to be there to see what to do and what not to do, as well as support that leader. It is not your job to make the lead do their job, it is your job to do your job! Think of David, in the time he could have exposed Saul, he didn't because He understood that at some point, God's hand was on him. God's hand is on you, sow the grace you want to get, and let God establish your goings.

COVERING

a) What does it mean to cover a leader?
b) Right is right and wrong is wrong, but what if my leader is wrong?
c) Is Covering or having a covering a part of God's plan?

ACTIVATION – In what ways do you think you can be a better covering to your leader, spouse or boss?

PRINCIPLE: Learn to figure out what your job is to the people you have been assigned to and do it God's way.

ASK YOURSELF: Did God tell me to submit to the people I have submitted to?

MEMORY VERSE: Genesis 9:23 – And Shem and Japheth took a garment, and laid it upon both their shoulders, and went backward, and covered the nakedness of their father; and their faces were backward and they saw not their father's nakedness.

REAL LIFE: If you are serving in ministry, you will get the opportunity to see the nakedness of leaders...keep them covered.

The story of Noah and his sons is an intense one, that would cause us to get into a discussion about a whole lot more than covering. Isn't it interesting that nobody had a problem or felt any kind of way about Noah being naked in his tent. It's probable that this is not the first time that this has happened. His son Ham went and told everybody and told them to come and see what dad was done. This is a very poor example of covering. The greatest example of covering is what God did in the Garden of Eden. The covering that God made was not because he NEEDED to cover them, but it was done because of the state that they found themselves in.

They were the ones that stated that they were naked, they were the ones that hid from God's voice/presence, and they were the ones that offered excuses for their failure to stand in the position that God had established them in. God set them up with jobs outside the garden, gave them instructions and made them a covering. He sacrificed the life of something else because of the state of their heart. You may at some point as a leader find yourself in a position to expose someone else's issues or to cover them. Just as God did in the garden of Eden, confront that issue and then cover them. This is not an excuse to allow sin to happen or to go on, this is about making sure that the heart of the individual is ministered to. If we jump to the new testament, we will see that the bible talks about the saints that are spiritual, restore them that have fallen...not expose them.

ADDRESSING ISSUES

a) What is the best way to approach something that you see in someone?
b) Is it my responsibility to address issues in leadership?
c) Sometimes it feels like nobody hears me, what do I do?
d) Sin Vs. personal faults

ACTIVATION – Explore ways to address issues that are building.

PRINCIPLE: What issues do I need to address in me before I address them in someone else?

ASK YOURSELF: Have I used all of my resources in order to address issues that I have been having?

MEMORY VERSE: 2 Samuel 12:7a – And Nathan said to David, Thou art the man.

REAL LIFE: There is always an honorable way to address issues to leadership and in your home.

This story is intense and details betrayal, murder and sabotage. This is the interesting part, the verse tells us that Nathan told David he was the man. You may want to look at the story and everything else that Nathan said and what David did. Nathan could have come to him as a prophet and said to him: God said you had this man killed, you took his wife and now God is angry cause you are in sin. He didn't' do that. When addressing negative issues, it is imperative that you figure out the best way so that the hearer hears it.

It is the rare heart of an individual that can be corrected by a subordinate or an equal (your friend or spouse), and still realize that they are supporting and loving you. The pride of many get's in the way. Here is the thing, if you believe that you have poured into me as a leader, or as a spouse that I have your back, then you would realize how difficult it has been for us to have this conversation from the beginning. At the same time, the way that I speak to you is going to determine how I hear and receive what you have to say.

There is a way to correct people without making it seem as if you are the one correcting them but that they are the ones receiving the correction that has penetrated their hearts. If you were working a job as the assistant manager, it is your job to make sure that everyone else is doing their job. If the general manager doesn't do their job, they may get in trouble but not by you. There's a way you could ask them for help that would highlight the fact that they have not been helping.

If we look at it with your spouse, we already know that nobody likes to be corrected especially by their spouse. Figure out a way to have a discussion with your spouse that isn't attacking and that they can hear that they need to adjust their behavior. You may be saying, I already have, well...try something different. As simple as that response is...try to do something else, cause clearly the way you have been going about it, hasn't worked.

THE NEED IS THE CALL

a) What have you been called to do?
b) What is the need on your job, in your house or in your local ministry?
c) You have been anointed to build the kingdom; how do you do that?
d) What is my position in active leadership?

ACTIVATION – What are some things that you do that does not fit into what you feel like you're called to?

PRINCIPLE: Your call is not diminished based on the job you do, but in the heart you do it in.

ASK YOURSELF: Has my calling gotten in the way of fulfilling a need?

MEMORY VERSE: Colossians 3:23 – And whatsoever you do, do it heartily, as unto the Lord and not unto men;

REAL LIFE: Service to the kingdom, is done to people, not a building and not a title.

This may be difficult for many to hear, but You have been anointed, but not anointed to "preach". You have been anointed to serve God in the kingdom, and he has regulated people to lead. It is our job to make sure that whatever we do, is done as if we are doing it for God. From your very existence, you have been given a purpose and destiny, locked on the inside of you, and it has remained your responsibility to make sure that you accomplish it by following God's direction.

Part of the way that is accomplished is done by the need in your local body. One of the largest issues in the world for me, is walking into a church service and all of the "big wigs" have stepped over a piece of paper, as if it wasn't their job. It speaks to a person's heart when the only thing that they are anointed to do, is only done when they are in front of people. The service of the kingdom doesn't start or end with people, it is in the facilitation of the kingdom. It is in the need. If I am needed to sing in the choir and I can sing...as prophetic as I am, I'm going to sing prophetically!!!

Ecc. 9:10, tells us that whatsoever your hands find to do, do it with your might, because there is nothing working in the grave. This scripture implies that your hands should be looking for something to do, instead of waiting on someone to call on you or give you position in order to accomplish the call He has placed on your life. Work with fervor, energy and drive that is in you. This is where you can understand that I'm called to the office of pastor, so let me pastor this bathroom. I'm called to preach the gospel, so let me preach to the mail man as I go and get the mail. The practical application of the spiritual things will bring greater understanding of said spiritual thing. At the end of the day, no matter what you are called to do, if there is a need in your local church, your home, or your job...that is the call. He's anointed you to be an answer...so answer the call!!!

d) Understanding the role of a leader
e) If you can't serve, can you lead.
f) If you desire the title for position only you will fail

ACTIVATION – Evaluate where you have been placed, and where you desire to go. Have you already been doing the work? If the answer to this question is no then you have work to do.

PRINCIPLE: Understanding that leaders are servants first.

ASK YOURSELF: Have I been doing the work of a true leader? Am I willing to serve while leading? Is it more about the title and less about the work?

MEMORY VERSE: Matthew 20:26—But among you it will be different. Whoever wants to be leader among you must be your servant.

REAL LIFE: If you can't be submitted and serve, you can't be committed and lead.

Leadership roles look luxurious and most people, often only understand the title and not the work that is required to lead. As a leader you aren't only accountable for you, but you are accountable for those connected to you. This means that you have to have the ability to understand serving in order to guide someone else. Without having the posture of a servant, you can't teach someone how to follow. Which then would make it hard to establish healthy relationships along with healthy boundaries. Heart of an intentional and true leader is the heart of a servant.

Being in charge means that you get dirtier than those you lead. You have to work to ensure that even the things that have been forgotten gets completed. This in itself shows how leadership isn't just delegating and occupying a seat of authority. You must be willing to get in the game and show that you aren't afraid of being in the thick of it with those that you support and lead. We see one of the best examples of leadership in Jesus. We see and understand that he hung in places where the commoners and sinners were. He did not shy away from that, but he went out to show that the environment nor the people controlled him, but that it was His heart and His desire to serve others. So, if Jesus could serve those who were unworthy how different are we?

Being a leader is more than a position it is a heart posture. If you can't serve how do you effectively lead. Don't just desire the position but desire to serve and build the people and elevation will come.

PERMISSION

d) Leading comes with responsibility.
e) Delegation comes with a grace. What is asked doesn't need explanation.
f) Appointed to lead causes access in places originally you would not have been granted

ACTIVATION – Identify the areas that you have been called to, what can you do to become a better leader?

PRINCIPLE: When being called to lead you have been given a grace, a permission to lead with the authority and integrity that the Father has given.

ASK YOURSELF: What areas have you been given access to that you may have overlooked?

MEMORY VERSE: Matthew 24:45-47 – A faithful, sensible servant is one to whom the master can give the responsibility of managing his other household servants and feeding them. If the master returns and finds that the servant has done a good job, there will be a reward. I tell you the truth, the master will put that servant in charge of all he owns.

REAL LIFE: It takes a true leader to have the grace and ability to access where God has called them while being humble enough to serve while leading.

When you are selected as a leader the assumption is that you have the ability to do the job that is assigned. There is often a grace to build and to cause development in others. With this you are appointed to be a delegator. You hand out task and you ensure that there is follow through, In order to do this you have had to be given permission and assignment by someone. How you use your permission is very important. As a leader you shouldn't mishandle those that you are leading. You should also take pride in taking the assignment given and exceeding what is expected of you. As a leader you have responsibilities that must be fulfilled and they can't always be delegated out. You are expected to show up even when things are bad. As our memory verse explains we are to be faithful and sensible servants as leaders. Being intentional shows those that you lead you were intended to lead them specifically as they can see how you are provoking and causing growth for them.

Having permission to lead causes there to be favor at each level. Leadership causes elevation and in that there are new things that you will have to tackle and overcome. The fact that you were committed and doing what you have been assigned causes a reward and that reward is promotion. Just when you think that what you have done has gone unnoticed you will find that the Father has already worked behind the scenes to open other doors in other areas. Now as a leader you have to have accomplished what you are intended to in order to progress forward. There is permission that is granted even when it comes to elevation that was intended for you. Your actions can cause delay in what was intended. For example, God sent you to a ministry to be the voice of hospitality, however you believe that the Lord has called you to pastor. Now neither of these have to be an untruth. Once you master serving in the house the Lord then has the ability to reward you. If you delay because you believe that you should be doing something different or something more grand you delay your access to your destiny.

PRODUCTION

d) What have you planted?
e) Are you producing after the heart of God?
f) Always working causes produced fruit. (1 Cor. 15:58)

ACTIVATION – Pray and ask the Lord what type of tree are you? What are you producing?

PRINCIPLE: Every leader produces fruit, good, bad or different speaks to the heart of the leader.

ASK YOURSELF: Am I reproducing? If so, what type of fruit am I producing?

MEMORY VERSE: 1 Peter 5:2-4
-
REAL LIFE: If you lead poorly you are creating more poor leaders.

The saying what is in you comes out is a very valuable statement. If you have a pure heart it is revealed, if you have a wicked heart it is reflected. What you give is often duplicated. In order to make sure that you are not planting the wrong type of tree you will get the wrong kind of fruit. You can attempt to pour into those that you are developing different than what is in your heart, but the root of your heart will show at some point. That is a poison that spreads. The next time your child or even your wife causes an issue or just gets on your nerves, think about what seeds you have planted within their boundaries and I guarantee you will be able to see how your behavior has now caused a root to form in those that you are connected to.

Have you taken on the heart of God or are you still stuck with your own heart and that is where you are feeding those that follow you from? If you haven't taken on the Heart of God you can cause more damage than good. Our hearts are deceitfully wicked, which means that we are creating more leaders that will be deceitfully wicked. So that you can make sure that your people are being built and not destroyed you will need to take on the heart and mind of God. When you build them from the heart of God you cause what you reproduce to be great.

When you are a leader you have to make sure that production never stops. This means that you have to ensure that you are continually working to perfect yourself and your heart so that you don't bleed on others and that you have the ability to cause your fruit to grow and be beneficial to someone else. You can also produce bad fruit depending on how you grow it. Be careful of the seeds you plant and where you plant them as you can see both the positive impacts and the negative impacts.

You can learn from both a good leader and a bad leader. One shows you what to do and the other shows you what not to do. When you are working to produce a harvest make sure that what you are planting with and watering with is beneficial to the soil and the seeds.

DEVELOPMENT

e) Leading with patience in order to build
f) Pulling the team to where you are.
g) You are only as strong as your weakest link

ACTIVATION – Who is the weakest link on your team? What have you done to assist them? Write down a list of things that you can do to cause your weakest link to become the strongest link.

PRINCIPLE: Leaders have to be disciplined in order to develop and equip their team. This takes versatility in leadership.

ASK YOURSELF: How do I help my team and myself to grow?

MEMORY VERSE: 1 Thessalonians 5:14 – And we urge you, brothers, admonish the idle, encourage the fainthearted, help the weak, be patient with them all.

REAL LIFE: Your ability to lead is based on your ability to understand and be flexible when you are trying to develop people beyond where they can see and even beyond where you may think they can go.

We understand that the level of responsibility for leaders can be overwhelming. Most times leaders aren't leading just one person. Having the ability to lead effectively comes from having the ability to deposit the vision into all that you lead regardless of their differences or biases.

As believers it is our responsibility to renovate our minds. The liberty of deliverance is the fact that you are no longer in bondage or controlled by what your mind tells you, but by the Spirit of God and His word. We talk about deliverance being about casting out demons, but that's just the beginning. As we continue our growth and development in the kingdom, we have to realize that even after the demon is gone, the bible shows us that it is our job to keep our house swept and clean.

Your house needs to be cleaned from top to bottom. How many of you have ever cleaned your house one time and stopped? Your house needs to be cleaned daily, so why would your house, your temple only needs to be cleaned by going to one seminar. Every opportunity to clean your house should be taken. Picking up little papers, washing the dishes, sweeping the floor, rearranging the room, all of those things are necessary. How, you may ask? Well, using the water of the word, worship and repentance, communion with God, worship and fellowship with the saints, forgiveness are tools we can use in order to keep our house clean. Like Captain Planet used to say: The power is yours!!!

My Leadership experience was one that was memorable and enjoyable. The expectation that is held for leaders that isn't always met would be that every leader is working to build a leader who can step into their role without error. A leader who doesn't struggle with who they are and the value they bring is normally the type of leader that wants to develop leaders like them to take over and feel the shoes of their present leader. Developing your team and pouring into each of them differently is required to have a successful team. Investing in their future is vital to who you are as a leader. If you can't confidently build a team of leaders who can do what you do, how you do it then what you have been commissioned to do will be unfulfilled. Our commission is to create disciples and if we aren't doing that we have missed the commission of Christ to us. So lead in order to develop.

FATHER

a) What is the responsibility of a father?
b) What did you not get from your father?
c) What is the authority that a father should walk in?
d) Are there any reflections of the Father that you can see in your father?

ACTIVATION – Pray for healing of those that have "father issues".

PRINCIPLE: You usually respond to God the way that you relate to your father.

ASK YOURSELF: Do I see God as father or an authority figure?

MEMORY VERSE: Matthew 6:9 – After this manner therefor pray ye: Our Father, which art in heaven, Hallowed be thy name.

REAL LIFE: Father is not just a title.

Culture will teach us that the responsibility of the father is no different than that of the mother. The parents are supposed to support each other. The only issue with that is that is not exactly how the bible describes it. Some of us may not really believe in roles in the relationship but the bible clearly shows us that the man is the headship of the family. That means that it is the responsibility of the of the father to think in advanced for the safety and protection of the family.

The relationship with the Father is going to usually be reflective of the relationship with the father. Think about it. The relationship that you have with your natural father can either be a support and open door to how you respond to your heavenly father. The absence of a father can make it even more difficult to approach and be open to your heavenly father.

The scripture used, is very specific. It details how we should approach our God. It is imperative that we see that he is first and foremost our Father. It identifies His title and position. Father is not just a title given to someone who produces a child but speaks to the position that they carry. The father is supposed to leave an inheritance to their children's children. He is the one who is smart enough to see beyond the now and see into the future for the sustenance of the family. The father waits for the wandering child to come home in order to place them back in their seat of authority and clothe them with dignity. The father is not one who just works and puts a roof over the head of the family, it is his job to be the head, be the roof. He covers them, protects them and stamps his identity on them, with something as simple as a name.

MOTHER

a) What is the responsibility of a mother?
b) What did you not get from your mother?
c) What is the authority that a mother should walk in?
d) What are the expectations that the mother should do?

ACTIVATION – Pray for healing of those that have "mother issues".

PRINCIPLE: Mother's produce based on the seed given to them.

ASK YOURSELF: My mother could only give what was given to her.

MEMORY VERSE: Proverbs 31:10 – Who can find a virtuous woman? For her price is far above rubies.

REAL LIFE: A mother is priceless to your development or destruction.

Mother's sometimes can get a bad rap. There is a story in Matthew about a mother that most only look at one line. She came to get help for her daughter. From the very beginning of this story, she was already in straights because she had to deal with her daughter who was in bondage. She came to Jesus asking if He could cast the demon out of her daughter. Mastering motherhood means understanding that she determined to do whatever it takes in order to secure freedom for her children. You may be thinking, my mom didn't do any of that. The truth is, her lack of doing, allowed you still to learn what not to do.

There's another story in Kings about a woman who was blessed prophetically with a child. The child ended up falling sick and ended up dying. She had not even asked for this baby, but the prophet of God had given her a reward for the room that he provided. The story continues that they were in the field, the boy's head is hurting, and the father says, take him to his mother. The mother went right to the one that provided the word that gave her the son. She said all is well, many would think that this was "in faith". What if she was so distraught, in grief she didn't know what to do. Grief will cause people to do a lot of things.

Mothers are always trying to figure out how to deal, with life and death. This is the great part, the end of the story the boy comes back to life, the boy got up. Because the woman went back to the place she made sacrifice for, the seed to come back to life. The son was the seed that was planted, and came back to life, but the mother is the one that carried it...celebrate her.

CHILDREN

a) Understanding the role of the child.
b) The silence of a child speaks volumes.
c) What influences are you giving your child?

ACTIVATION – Examine if you are allowing God to be a parent for you...

PRINCIPLE: I am a child of God is not just a positive statement...be a child.

ASK YOURSELF: Am I trying to parent God, or being his child?

MEMORY VERSE: Proverbs 31:28a – Her children arise up and call her blessed;

REAL LIFE: Children are a blessing from the Lord, but can be difficult if we don't know our role and responsibilities.

This is one of the funny things that we have a study on. The behavior of the child, the attitude of the child or children is not usually discussed in scripture. There are few churches that have discussions on the heart of the child except for children should be seen and not heard. There was a time this was the principle; children do not need to have an opinion and the opinion that we they have should be given to them. Here is the thing, this scripture talks about how the children will arise up and call her blessed.

In order for the child to arise up and call her blessed, that means that the child had to be down at some point. As the bible described the attitude of the child through scripture, we see their dependence on the parent as well as their development because of the parent. It is the parents that continue to develop and minister to the child. The child develops based on the influence of the parentals and their social environment.

Jesus said that unless we have the heart of a child, we won't enter the kingdom. This is about the heart of a child that is dependent on God. I know you were expecting that we were going to be talking about the role and responsibility of the child, and we are, the child of God has the same responsibility. The interdependence on the father, the trust and obedience that says whatever your choices are, I know you want the best for me. The child should be protected and defended. The Lord is defending you, standing for you, teaching you and will turn the world upside down to protect you, and your job is to play safe in His arms.

FAMILY

a)   What is the role of the family in the kingdom?
b)   The family of God vs natural family.
c)   How am I pouring into my family?

ACTIVATION – Describe the structure of your family

PRINCIPLE: Every family has a structure and order, and it doesn't have to look like anyone elses.

ASK YOURSELF: Am I reflecting the family of God, or the Joneses?

MEMORY VERSE: Hebrews 3:4 – For every house is built by some man; but he that built all things is God.

REAL LIFE: God is the architect of every house and family. Trust Him for your design.

There are several different kinds of family. You have natural born family, meaning the family that you were born into. Then you have the family you picked. The family of God is universal, not worldwide. We stop at the fact that our family are people that we can see. You have family that you live with, family in your nucleus and then people that are distant. You also have family that are just not in your circle that you don't know about until you show up at the family reunion. I remember going to a family reunion and seeing people so light skinned that I thought they were white. They seemed to have a whole other culture; they didn't say yes ma'am and yes sir. They didn't come immediately when a parent called. They had an opinion when the grown-ups were talking. We were not supposed to have a voice among adults.

This is the way we have to see the family that we have and the family of God. No matter if we are talking about the family that God has given us, or if it is the family of God, OTHER SHEEP I HAVE WHICH ARE NOT OF THIS FOLD, is what Jesus said. What does that mean? There were people that were doing everything the disciples were. They were part of their crew, some of them were of John's crew, they were still baptizing for remittance of sin, they were what we would call old school. This is where we have to realize that there are people that do not do what we do, respond how we respond, even to each other in the family. The best part is this, even if they are my family, they don't have to be structured the way that we are.

If you look at many families that look like mine, (African American) you will see that the father or the man has the run of the house, brings home the bacon and establishes the function of the house. The truth is my wife makes more money than I do, she's better at money management than I am, but I know how to spend it. This is how our house is structured. We work together as partners as a team. Does that mean that we don't have a head to our family...no, not at all it just doesn't look like yours. God is the one that is building it...keeping it growing...I'll follow his plan and structure, not yours. lol

WHO ARE YOU??

a) I am a friend of God
b) Responsibility as a friend of God
c) No longer a servant but friend

ACTIVATION – Take a moment and ask the Father who/what He has designed you to be? Does this align with who you believe you are? If this doesn't align what can you do to ensure that you are headed toward God's plan and not just your own plan.

PRINCIPLE: The Lord framed me in His image and likeness therefore I AM!!

ASK YOURSELF: How do I identify who I am now God destined me to be?

MEMORY VERSE: John 15:15 – Henceforth I call you not servants; for the servant knoweth not what his lord doeth: but I have called you friends; for all things that I have heard of my Father I have made known unto you.

REAL LIFE: The Lord created us in his likeness and image and has chosen us to be more than servants, but also His friends.

When you think of friendship how do you quantify who you choose as a friend? Reading in John shows us that we were qualified as friend by doing what was commanded of the Lord. With this understanding it allows us to understand that when we defy what has been commanded would be the times that our Father is not pleased and we then can't be considered friend in the midst of our disobedience. We have to acknowledge our short fall and repent. This is a common way that we often handle our earthly relationships. When someone does something that you have not asked or that you have spoke against that is now a chapter you are looking to close or isolate from. How would you feel if that was the approach that God took with you?

We have to understand that as God has called us friend there are assignments attached to the relationship that we have with our Father. As a friend of God there is still the responsibility of following the commandments and honoring the agreement that you agreed to. Separating what you may expect from your friend from what God may expect from you would be a double standard. Often the relationship that we have with God should be reflective of our expectations of others. You expect loyalty, honesty and sacrifice from your friend, but you aren't willing to give those things to God. Remember He calls us friend so we are responsible to keep His commands.

Think of ways that you can improve your friendship with God.

WHO HAVE THEY MADE YOU??

a) Allowing the words of others to define you
b) Removing who the world sees you as and putting on who you were created to be
c) Who He made me not who they say I am!
d) ACTIVATION – Remove the mask of who people have expected you to be and put on the heart and mind of God intended for you. Identify the areas that you have just owned because you felt obligated to people. Remove the toxic or unhealthy characteristics that you have hidden behind because you were uncertain of your identity.

PRINCIPLE: The Lord framed me in His image and likeness therefore I AM!!

ASK YOURSELF: How do I identify who I am now, versus who God destined me to be?

MEMORY VERSE: Genesis 1:27 – So God created man in his own image, in the image of God created he him; male and female created he them.

We often think of what we want to do and how we want to do it and not necessarily what we have been designed to do. We often listen to what others have said or what we believe we are connected to versus consulting the Father about our direction. When you think about where you have been what things have you accepted as a part of you that you can identify that God may not have intended for you. Have you accepted the word assignments of others? Many of the actions and identities you have taken on have come from the words of others and not what you were created to be.

The Lord made you in His likeness and in His image. Have you ever wondered then where does the other stuff come from? Often times we take on the characteristics of those around us and what we digest into our systems. We allow the words of man to form us beyond what God has done. We allow what we see in the media to shape us versus what God has already downloaded into us. What this shows is that we allow many different entities to speak into who we are. We limit our potential when we only invest in what we think or what others think. The word tells us that he knew us in our mother's womb and that he already knew the plans and thoughts he had toward us. That means that he took time with our creation. He invested in us only for us to then say that what he has done wasn't enough. This is where pride steps in. How dare we accept the worlds of those who don't even have the ability to control themselves and yet we doubt the creator of all. Be invested in finding out who God made you and who He destined you to be versus assuming the title of those around you that have no vested interest.

The Father created you to do a work in the earth. He made you special and uniquely you for a reason. Stop attempting to fit into the molds of other people. Work to identify who God created you to be and use that as your platform to build the kingdom. You are a kingdom assigned citizen and you have been commissioned to the work that the Father has placed in you.

Pray and ask God who He made you to be and what task has he called you to.

WHO HE SAYS YOU ARE?

a) I am a child of God
b) I am redeemed and justified
c) I am an heir

ACTIVATION Team up with a partner and ask God who does He say you are and who does he say your partner is, also ask him what is it that He wants you to sacrifice in order to live out what has been set for your life.

PRINCIPLE: You were designed to be who God says you are not what the world has tried to make you!!

ASK YOURSELF: How do I identify what God has made me versus what I have allowed myself to become?

MEMORY VERSE: John 1:12 – But as many as received him, to them gave he power to become the sons of God, even to them that believe on his name

REAL LIFE: Understanding that what God has said concerning to you matters more than what you think of yourself and what others may think. Your false humility is often rooted in pride and causes stagnation to the gifts that are waiting to be used.

Often times the reason you miss who you are in God is because we often don't understand who we were created to be. You get so used to just accepting what is said about you that you don't take the *time* to invest in who you were created to be. Existing only in what someone has declared about you and not what the Father has said limits your ability to see and or be who you were designed to be for the world. You must first understand that you are first a child of God. This alone makes you an heir to the kingdom. Without this understanding you live beneath where you have been called. Understanding that the Father has given you a grace and an authority because you are His child. This permits you access to places and things you wouldn't normally qualify for.

In addition to being a child of God you are redeemed and justified. Although, we are imperfect and striving to be more like our Father He has already redeemed and justified you. You are no longer fighting to be free but have a right to be free and not limited to your past or the boundaries that you have even set for yourself. One of the biggest issues that cause believers to be stuck in the old shell is the inability to identify the boundaries that you have set for yourself. God has spoken that you are only for you to work hard at not being what or who you were made to be. God made us the head and not the tail, the lender and not the borrower, all why you are setting up hurdles that block you from being what He has said about you.

You may have lost sight of who God made you to be. In order for you to get back into the swing of things you will have to get in your word and spend time studying. You won't know what has been said about you without getting into the face of your heavenly father and reading His word. The exploration of what people say should never be your sole focus. Leave room enough to identify who you have been called and purposed to be.

Take the remaining days left in this week and ask God who He made you to be? Ask Him what steps you need to take to get to this place? Don't miss purpose because you haven't taken the time to identify who you are.

WHO IS HE??

a) He is the creator
b) He is all knowing
c) He is our savior.

ACTIVATION – With a partner make a list individually of who God is, after writing out your list compare list and see what things you missed that would apply. Pray with your partner that you both have the ability to see God and all that He is to you. Pray that you never take God for granted and that you always Honor who He is and who He made you to be.

PRINCIPLE: God is our healer, deliverer, savior, and all that we need He encompasses and provides to all of His children!!

ASK YOURSELF: Have I acknowledge who God is in my life and in the lives of those that I am connected to?

MEMORY VERSE: John 1:1-3 –In the beginning was the Word, and the Word was with God, and the Word was God. He was in the beginning with God. All things came into being through Him, and apart from Him nothing came into being that has come into being.

REAL LIFE: God is more than what you give Him credit for. God is sovereign. His power is infinite, and His love covers, and He is your keeper.

God is sovereign. He is the same yesterday, today and forever. The extent of who God is for each person can at times vary. Depending on the season and where you are in life often determines what you see Him as for you. There are the foundational components that exist always. He is the creator of all things. This shows how powerful and mighty He is. God isn't a deadbeat dad He is the father that makes things happen for His children. He knows the entire plan for your life. This is how He allows you to be able to conquer whatever arises in your life because He knows how strong you are. He knows every obstacle before it ever reaches you. His sovereignty transcends from heaven to earth. This is how He holds everything and everyone together.

God is also our savior, and in Him saving the world it causes Him to then be so many things. He is your healer, deliverer, provider, mind regulator, your heavy load sharer and a host of other titles that causes your life to be able to be sustained without compromise. God shows up in every situation to ensure that the sacrifice He made of His only begotten son was not in vain. Often Christians trap God into what they believe He can be or what they have experienced Him being. Taking the bible for face value allows your common mind to understand who He is and what that means for you. Everything the bible says about Him is true. There are no errors or mistakes. He wants to have you prosper as your soul prospers. You just have to allow Him to be who the bible says He is.

WHERE ARE YOU??

a) I am seated in heavenly places
b) With each level of faith He grants you access to places you would have never imagined
c) I am at the heart of the King

ACTIVATION – Close your eyes and vision a place where you go to meet the Father. Where are you? What is the Father saying to you in this place? Was there anything significant about where you are? Ask the Father where He wants you to go.

PRINCIPLE: I am where my Father is and have been granted access to heavenly realms to be closer to His heart and mind!!

ASK YOURSELF: Is where I am where God has called me? If it isn't, how do I get to where He desires me to be?

MEMORY VERSE: Ephesians 2:6 – and raised *us* up together and made *us* sit together in the heavenly *places* in Christ Jesus.

REAL LIFE: Where I am may not be where I am called to be but I have the ability to get to where I need to be based on my commitment to my purpose.

Often times you have to check your heart and your position. You can think that things are okay and that you are s you to that everything that we do is in faith. The moment your faith stops is the moment you are no longer moving the way that God wants you to move but you are moving under the stagnation of what you have limited for your own progress. You should always live at the heart of God. This allows you to make sure that you are in the right place and in the will of God versus doing your own thing. Without faith how do you know that where you are is where God wants you to be. If you don't ask Him where he wants you, how do you know where you should be? You are given the freedom to choose, however when you are called and you rebel versus submitting there are consequences. Your location is vital. If you are in the wrong place you don't have the ability to do the assignment you are called to. There was a period where due to hurt I chose to leave Detroit and went to another place. Originally I didn't see anything wrong with my location.

I still attended church and I was still working to become what the Lord had purposed. I did ministry however the Lord had to remind me that the place I was in was not the place I had been called to. He literally caused me to go back to the place I started out in so that He could heal me but so that I could also be a healing agent to those where I had left. They had need of the purpose that God had placed inside of me and me being in a place that I wasn't called to wasn't going to get done what was needed. By now you may be wondering how am I seated in heavenly places when I am now talking about earthly locations. Being seated in heavenly places speaks to us being at the heart of God. Carrying out His plan is so much easier when you are in your place and in the proper seat.

NOUN

a) What is a soul tie?
b) Is there scripture that talks about soul ties?
c) Is it possible to be have a positive soul-tie?

ACTIVATION – Break ungodly soul ties.

PRINCIPLE: Soul ties, are not just people but can be any noun, (person, place or things).

ASK YOURSELF: Am I being controlled by anything above God?

MEMORY VERSE: John 8:32 – And ye shall know the truth, and the truth shall make you free.

REAL LIFE: There is nothing wrong with loving and supporting people and things, be careful to keep God on the throne of your heart.

In school we learned what a noun was, and it is a person, place or thing. When operating in life, you have to realize and be conscience of the fact that we make connections to all kinds of things and people. Many times, people only discuss soul ties as it pertains to people and sex. Soul-ties extend to more than just people, but to things as well. You may be asking how? Well, have you ever been driving in your old neighborhood and started to talk to someone about when you used to live there? All of those memories start coming back and it's almost as if you are reliving that moment, positive and negative, you have a soul tie to that place.

I remember I had a ring that I didn't have a soul tie to, but the person that gave me the ring had one. They were adamant about getting that ring back because it was a parent's ring before it was given to me. They were heartbroken more over the ring than the end of the relationship, enough to file a lawsuit regarding it. When you start making moves over material things, or emotional stances in order to make sure you keep that thing close to you, you know that it's a soul tie. The basic definition of a soul tie is something that you are connected to through your soul (mind, will and emotions).

This is why most of the time people mention how sex creates a soul tie, as it does, but we minimize it's effects when we only see sexual soul ties. You can have a soul tie with a place, a church, an organization. Anything that your emotions connect to when you're not there is a soul tie. It becomes a bondage and something that needs to be broken when that soul tie starts coming in front of God. If your best friend calls you in the middle of service or prayer, and you are willing to leave, break the ungodly soul tie, because you've moved them into the place of God in your heart.

MANIFESTATIONS

a) What are some ways to recognize a soul tie?
b) What are some identifiable soul ties in the world now?
c) Godly and ungodly soul ties, look the same

ACTIVATION – Understand and acknowledge soul ties between groups of people.

PRINCIPLE: Soul ties will manifest in your emotions as well as physically in front of you.

ASK YOURSELF: My heart connects are seen in how I respond to them, how am I responding?

MEMORY VERSE: Ephesians 1:18a – The eyes of your understanding being enlightened;

REAL LIFE: Many times, what we see in front of us is a manifestation of something that is happening in the spirit or seeping through your emotions.

It is very easy to look at someone and think you know what's wrong with them or what's happening in them. Have you ever had an attitude and someone close to you knew it and you kept trying to pretend or hide that you were upset about something because you didn't want to talk about it? This is what we refer to as a manifestation. It is the uncovering of something that is covered or hidden underneath something else.

Many times, our reactions are either based on our godly response, demonic or something from our soul (emotional). According Inc.com, 95% of purchases happen because of unconscious choices and emotionally inspired reasons. What does that mean? That we are driven more by our emotions in making purchases, that's not demonic that's emotional. If we use that same thinking, we will be able to see that many of the reasons we stay in relationships that are unhealthy, or in relationships that are healthy is because we either get or don't get what we need emotionally from those that we are in relationship with.

We see soul tie connections in the BLM (Black Lives Movement), though we don't all aspire to the movement, there are things that they stand for that are substantial. However, we can see how people will have a connection to the organization of BLM, and not really understand their roots, what their goals or focuses are. People are on the streets fighting with and for them because it is BLM. There are some who are attached to a religious organization or idea. This is why behaviors are looked over that are negative because there is a soul tie connection there, and the manifestation is seen in ignoring that behavior.

https://www.inc.com/logan-chierotti/harvard-professor-says-95-of-purchasing-decisions-are-subconscious.html

GODLY/UNGODLY

a) What's the difference?
b) How do I know I'm operating in either one?
c) Is this connection or tie leading to grace or detriment?

ACTIVATION – Understand and acknowledge soul ties between groups of people.

PRINCIPLE: There is a clear difference between Godly and Ungodly soul ties, it's based in doing.

ASK YOURSELF: Is my response to my "soul tie", godly or ungodly, this is how I can tell what it is.

MEMORY VERSE: 1 Samuel 18:1 – Now when he had finished speaking to Saul, the soul of Jonathan was knit to the soul of David, and Jonathan loved him as his own soul.

REAL LIFE: Got to understand the difference because one needs to be fostered the other needs to be cut off.

One of the things that we have to understand, is that if there is a negative there is a positive. While dealing with something as sensitive as soul ties, we have to remember that if there is an ungodly soul tie, there is a godly soul tie. There is a connection based on the mind, will and emotions that you can have with people that is building and pushes you into greatness with God. The purpose of the godly soul-tie is based on the establishment and upbuilding of the kingdom. All the way from Genesis, God made it clear that we it is not good for us to be alone. He connects us with people in order to build the kingdom.

Have you ever been sitting in a service and looked at your friend or pastor for that matter, and had a whole conversation without saying a word? You guys are cracking up, or ready to go and minister to the same person or realize this person who just got ministry needs more ministry and you guys are both ready to go and minister. This is where you can see the godly soul tie. The bible talks about how we should provoke each other to good works, the person with that connection can do it faithfully and build each other.

The ungodly soul tie does not produce growth in your character or behavior, it is usually set to produce something out of the soul. The ungodly soul tie is not about producing it's about selfishness and making sure that you feel good. The ungodly soul tie and connection will always set you up to feel, good, bad or indifferent. The ungodly soul tie will always be about stimulation and self focused. The ungodly soul tie with a person will cause you to maintain an attitude with someone who has treated them wrong, and not talk to that friend about restoration and healing. What you sow you reap, so if you sow into that soul tie, you will reap from that soulish stimulation.

FREEDOM

a) How can I get free from a soul tie?
b) What does freedom from a soul tie look like?
c) What is the process of freedom from soul ties?

ACTIVATION – Break ungodly soul ties.

PRINCIPLE: Freedom from anything, comes with commitment to not be tied to it again.

ASK YOURSELF: Do I *really* want to be disconnected from this soul tie or connection?

MEMORY VERSE: John 8:36 – Therefore if the Son makes you free, you shall be free indeed

REAL LIFE: Freedom from soul ties is as easy as a sentence, staying free is about practice.

Here we are, freedom from soul ties. This is the real question. How do we get free from a soul tie? How do we work ourselves into getting away from the bondage of an ungodly soul tie, commitment or connection? Well, it really is as simple as a sentence in order to break the soul tie, but to maintain it's separation takes practice. You have to work out the rest of that. As you break soul ties, you have to remember that that connection has been there for a day or 5 years. Your soul has created a connection and something that would not just go away. I mean that there is an addiction to it in our soul.

Breaking it is the first part, it's kind of like phantom pain. Even after a leg is gone sometimes you can feel pain as if it is still there, because the mind has been convinced that it is there. It has to be "tricked" in a sense to realize that it's not there anymore. Take a look at this: As God sets you free you have to realize the meaning of all of this. Let's look at the specifics of that scripture (the memory verse).

If the Son makes you free, this word free means more than just delivered from bondage or a prison. It means to liberate or to make exempt. To make you exempt from the penalty of that bondage or from the power of that bondage. When he sets you free from a soul tie, he eliminates the bondage of and the penalty of it. The rest of that say that you are free indeed. This is the preaching part. This means that you are no longer a slave, no longer obligated and unrestrained in truth; and the truth makes you free!!!

The bible shows us that this process of freedom from soul ties eliminates us from the penalty of soul ties. This isn't heaven or hell; it is about having to deal with everyday life and how to manage it. You don't have to live in ANY kind of bondage that you have lived in, because he is CONSTANTLY, setting you free!!!!

GLORY

a) The manifestation of His presence
b) The weight of His glory
c) The purpose of His glory

ACTIVATION – Take 15 minutes a day this week and invite the glory of the Lord into your prayer space. Write down what He speaks or what he instructs you to do.

PRINCIPLE: The representation of glory in the earth is the understanding of God being present in the midst of His people!!

ASK YOURSELF: How do I identify God's glory being present?

MEMORY VERSE: John 1:14 – And the Word was made flesh, and dwelt among us, (and we beheld his glory, the glory as of the only begotten of the Father,) full of grace and truth.

REAL LIFE: The glory of God is like everything else in the kingdom. Activated based on our faith. You have the ability to see it and respond to it based on your faith.

Often seeing the glory of God can often be seen as someone being deep or too spiritual. That can be said in relation to many things. However, we understand that as a believer we activate and operate in faith and that is what causes God to move and that is how we can then see His glory. Looking at our memory verse it says the Word was made flesh, notice word was capitalized and the reason it was is because that is the indicator that the word in this sentence is reflective of God being the Word. The Word was made flesh meaning He then was in human form dwelling in our midst. His presence is significant of His glory. Him showing up and being in the midst of the people was His display of who He was. When we look at the weight of glory this is His presence and power filling the place and overtaking the people. Again another act in faith but this also can align with your measures of praise. The weight of His glory filling a room can be based on how bad the believer is in need of an infilling and how big their faith is that God will show up based on their faith and desire.

His glory can also be seen in reverence and honor of His dwelling amongst His children. As a kingdom kid we have the privilege and the extreme honor of being partakers in the basking of His glory. We have direct access to invite His glory into any place that we enter and or dwell. Gods sovereignty allows His glory to free course and reign amongst believers with faith. There are also experiences of His glory where you can see glory dust, a fog of glory and it all identifies His reign in the earth for His children and heirs to the kingdom.

WIND

a) The sound of wind
b) The power of wind to cause shifting
c) The wind of the spirit different than the wind of your flesh

ACTIVATION – Pray and ask God to move in the wind and show you His hand.

PRINCIPLE: Although you can't physically see wind it can be one of the strongest things you feel !!

ASK YOURSELF: How do I recognize the wind of God in my life?

MEMORY VERSE: John 3:8 – The wind blows where it wishes and you hear the sound of it, but do not know where it comes from and where it is going; so is everyone who is born of the spirit.

REAL LIFE: Wind an attribute that we can't see but that we feel often. Wind is an element that can cause something to be moved into the correct place or out of place. As a believer you have to be in the right position when the wind comes so that you are not blown out of position.

Wind is another symbol of the glory of God. It is something that you can't see but you can definitely feel it. You can sense it bit you can't tangibly touch it. Often in the spirit when you feel the wind it is notification that it is time to move. It is indicated in scripture that wind at times was a sign or indication of when God wanted someone to move or a sign that it was time to do what they were supposed to do. Wind is a powerful sign without being able to be seen. You can hear wind blowing, strong winds can knock you off your post. Winds sometimes can be a signal to an upcoming storm. So, the significance of wind can be an indication of different things but most often it is an attempt to prepare or notify you of what is to come. Even when it came to the day of Pentecost they described it as a mighty rushing wind. This signifies that the wind was hurried but also full of power. Another sign of something mighty happening. We take many things for granted but the ability to understand the move coming and being required is significant.

Being able to be sensitive to the wind so that you can understand what needs to happen is an important component. The force of the wind could be to force you into the place that God has been trying to get you to willingly go. The wind comes not to harm you but to allow you to be shifted. This shift can bring elevation, correction or redirection. Although natural wind also can move things it's importance isn't as strong as the wind of God. This wind is powerful and often necessary for preparation and cultivation even of the ground so that the seeds sown can begin to grow.

Pray and ask God to reveal to you when the wind is blowing in your life if it is for a shift or if it is to increase your spiritual authority. As the wind also represents a form of God's glory it could also be to intensify your anointing and your call.

RAIN

a) Withholding the rain
b) Releasing the rain
c) Growth because of the rain

ACTIVATION – Pray for rain in the areas that you have sown and see what begins to grow. Don't take anything for granted every area where there is growth, or advancement document and see how God releases rain for you.

PRINCIPLE: There are times that a drought will come and then there are times that rain will be released and potentially flood the land but it is all in timing and purpose!!

ASK YOURSELF: Have I caused the Lord to hold back the rain in areas of my life that need it?

MEMORY VERSE: Leviticus 26:4 – Then I shall give you rains in their season, so that the land will yield its produce and the trees of the field will bear their fruit..

REAL LIFE: Rain causes things to grow, the wetness may cause discomfort, but the finished product is worth the discomfort.

Rain is another form of God's glory. It is one of the forms that we have the ability to see, feel and touch. The difference for rain and as the memory verse would state rain happens year round but is normally more consistent based on the season. There are seasons in our lives where based on our lack of faith or disobedience God may have to hold back the rain and allow a drought to occur to get our attention. As we see throughout scripture there were a few dry spells that caused crops to die because they didn't have the rain to keep them growing. This happens to many of us in ministry we are often caught in our own way and then there comes the drought. When the drought comes we are now n distraught and not understanding the why when it has been our hand and stagnation that has caused us to be in this place. You will have the ability to rebuild after the drought but there are things that you can potentially lose that you needed.

Once the rain that was held up is released you then have the ability to start your crop all over. The Lord will cause the rain to be what you need for things to grow and get back in order. The one thing you want to acknowledge during this time is that the season for you to grow is now so don't delay when the rain comes. Remember it may be wet and even cold while you must labor but the labor will all be for purpose and will payoff in harvest after while. Often you may get distracted by the rain and the discomfort it may bring but understand that now isn't the time to quit. Now is the time to do the work. Everybody wants the harvest but not the work. You can't reap what you haven't sown. So when the rain comes be ready to do what is your portion so that when harvest time does come you aren't experiencing a drought.

There is also the rain of God's glory. There are times when you are in worship or in prayer and praise to God and you will then feel Him begin to pour out rain on you. This rain is different it is a sign of His glory and this rain is filling you up. This rain causes growth in your spirit and in your intimacy with the Father. Be able to understand the rain of glory so that you can get an infilling from the Lord so that you are never empty.

FIRE

a) Refining Fire
b) The fire of the Holy Spirit
c) Consumed by His fire

ACTIVATION – Ask the Lord to refine you through fire.

PRINCIPLE: Fire comes to purify and purge out, while at the same time causing new levels to be opened!!

ASK YOURSELF: How do I allow the refiners fire to continually refine me without resistence?

MEMORY VERSE Hebrews 12:29 – For our God is a consuming fire.

REAL LIFE: Fire doesn't feel good and often times causes resistance, but it is necessary and causes one to be permanently changed.

Fire is intended to cause perfection to things. Many valuable things start off in one form and must go into the fire in order to be made what it was ultimately intended to be. Fire is something as believers many would want to avoid as it is very uncomfortable and often a challenge to stay in the fire. The thing of it is if you knew the end result would you be in that fire. See knowing that once I go through the fire and come out the imperfections that once was will no longer be often causes people to bypass fear and be willing to go through the process. The fire of the Holy Spirit burns away and causes accountability so that the struggle doesn't have to continue but can be addressed and corrected. Fire is hot so it isn't the thing you want to do but understanding that it is a temporary catastrophe in order for long term changes and growth which make the fire now worth it. Evaluating the benefits of what happens it changes your heart. Now fire can also be a sign of glory. Similar to rain it is one that we can see, touch, and hear. The glory of fire can be when the power of God hits you and it is trimming away the battle wounds by refining you in the fire of the Holy Spirit in the form of praise. You have to be able to recognize that there are signs of glory and also work being done in and through an individual.

The fire of the Holy Ghost should be all consuming. It should be the thing that will cause you to yield all that you are to the Father. The fact that you are consumed with His fire should identify to you that there is something in you that He desires to get out of you. Each experience may not be the all consuming fire and may simply be indicative of what He wants to do for you. So make sure that you are centered and prepared for the fire so that you don't have to go back through the process when it already is an uncomfortable place to be. If you look at the signs of glory you should be able to understand that the Lord wants our attention and He will go about getting it by any means necessary.

HEALTHY BOUNDARIES

a) Learning how to say no.
b) Boundaries are designed to protect us.
c) If boundaries can be healthy they can also be unhealthy.

ACTIVATION – Name some things/people that you have difficulty saying no to.

PRINCIPLE: Establishing healthy boundaries are logically and spiritual.

ASK YOURSELF: Are the boundaries that I have set healthy or unhealthy?

MEMORY VERSE: Psalms 74:17 – Thou has set all the boundaries of the earth; thou hast made summer the winter.

REAL LIFE: If there are no boundaries the city...you...have no protection.

As this year continues, I'm sure there have been people that you have encountered that you have had a difficult time saying no to. From family and friends to even bosses. Setting boundaries is healty and keeps you preserved to grow and prosper. Here is where we have to be careful. Some of our boundaries have been established based on our previous trauma. There are things that we choose to not do because of the fear of things that may happen or based on the experiences that we have encountered. These would-be unhealthy boundaries. These are the kind of boundaries that we set that keep everyone out. These are actually principalities.

Remember Rapunzel, she was put into a tower to be protected from the rest of the world. It was because of the fear of her mom (who actually turned out to be a witch), who was injured by something that happened in her life. What happened to her. She lived so long in that tower that her hair was long enough for someone to climb up it. The things is this, she was protected from the world but she also locked EVERYONE out. Even the people who were sent to rescue her. It took her to break through the unhealthy boundaries.

It is imperative that we recognize that boundaries are needed, and are designed by God in order to protect us and to keep us safe, at the same time our establishment of boundaries cannot be based on our fear or intimidation of the words of people. Trusting that God will be the one who establishes them and that He does it to show His love and protection is necessary.

SAY NO

a) No is not a bad word.
b) Do you have a difficult time telling people no?
c) What are some tools you can use, when you know you need to say no?

ACTIVATION – Give some tools to help each other to say no.

PRINCIPLE: Healthy boundaries allow you to say no, and no feel bad about it.

ASK YOURSELF: Am I always saying yes, because I don't want to disappoint people?

MEMORY VERSE: Matthew 5:37 – But let your communication be year, year: Nay, nay: for whatsoever is more than these cometh of evil.

REAL LIFE: Sometimes saying no, is difficult because we find identity in pleasing people.

There is something to us wanting to be appreciated by people. There's nothing wrong with us wanting to make our friends and family happy, but when we have replaced people with God, we have a problem I know some of you are trying to figure out how you could replace God with people. That's actually pretty easy. Some of you work so hard to make sure that people are pleased that God is not your focus. You're working so hard to make sure that you prove to people what you can do that it is no longer about pleasing God, it's about proving them wrong.

Learning when and how to say no will set you free. If you are working all day, come home to clean and cook for your family and a friend calls you and ask you to do something, it's ok to say no or that you'll get it done the next day. Is heaven going to close because you don't jump for every person that calls? Are you going to be dropped into the bowls of hell because you said no. Understanding when and how to set boundaries will allow you to be freed from the opinions of people and pushed into a place of surrender to God that goes beyond the bondage of pleasing people.

People pleasing will cause you to ignore your prayer time. It will make you forget about reading your bible in order to run someone to the mall. People pleasing will cause bitterness and anger to fester in your heart because nobody has appreciated what you have been doing for them. Learning how to say no saves you from more than being used, it preserves you from bitterness, unforgiveness and resentment. The tongue is a little member that can set a large fire, let that fire sthat is set be based on a no, that purifies your motives.

BUILD A BRIDGE

a) What have you been having an issue getting over?
b) Disappointments will come, but have you been able to work through them?
c) Offenses are the bait of Satan and will cause you to be stuck and not cross over into greatness.

ACTIVATION – See those things that you have not gotten over in your hands, give them over to God.

PRINCIPLE: Simply, GET OVER IT!

ASK YOURSELF: What have I been holding on to, because of what someone has done to me?

MEMORY VERSE: Luke 17:1 – Then said he unto the disciples, It is impossible but that offenses will come, but woe unto him through whom they come!

REAL LIFE: People will do all kinds of things, it is your job to find your footing and not be moved.

The memory verse is clear in this scripture, basically that offenses will come. As a matter of fact the scripture continues to tell us that it would be better that a large lime stone that was used for grinding be tied around their necks than to cause such an offense to one of His little ones. I mean, He goes in about how he feels about people who causes offense to His people. But by verse 3, his response and the responsibility for his people becomes the focus. Think about and focus on yourself.

Jesus was really clear about what our response should be to offense. He will take care of the things that people are doing, it was our job to rebuke, if we offended, repent and then forgive. There is no in-between. Then he went even further, and said if they offend you seven times in a day and if they repent, again, forgive them, again!!

Jesus was clear about what our responses should be upon offense. If we do not build a bridge we will never cross over into the place where authority is released. Why would that be the thing? Forgiveness is the thing that leads you to apostolic freedom. The next thing that is said in these scriptures is that the apostles said...The apostles, was not what he started with. They were called disciples. Forgiveness releases the authority of the supernatural into your life...so, if you want to see the supernatural, build a bridge and get over it.

PERMISSION GRANTED

a) Have you given God permission to protect you?
b) Is Jesus your protection?
c) He will teach you how to stand on his word as protection.

ACTIVATION – Pray and yield to God's ability to take care of you.

PRINCIPLE: You don't have to always be so defensive...Let God be God.

ASK YOURSELF: Are you always ready to fight?

MEMORY VERSE: Psalms 62:6 – He only is my rock and my salvation: he is my defense; I shall not be moved.

REAL LIFE: You have to allow God to defend you.

Sara, was a lady in the old testament that was old and promised that she was going to have a baby. Her husband was older than her. When the angel of the Lord showed up to tell him, she laughed. She then decided to take things into her own hands and have somebody else sleep with her husband in order to have the baby. She got upset and started picking on the lady because Abram, treated her different. The story goes that she got pregnant and still ended up kicking the lady out of their camp and God stepped in and took care of that kid.

Here is the revelation, She could have saved her some time, by not stepping into it and allowing God to just be God. We continue to say that we trust God, but we only trust him as far as we can see him. I mean unless we can see him moving, we don't trust him and we take on the title of God and get to work, based on what he said. We don't war with the prophesies; we go to war and start fighting to MAKE it happen instead of following His instructions.

The best defense that we have is God. He is not just my defense; he is my rock. He is the thing I can stand on and trust. When the world comes and tries to create an image of who I am, God makes sure that he jumps up and stands in the way so that we are not blown over and shifted based on the winds of the world. When people rose against David, he leaned on God...He got direction. He trusted what He said and followed His instructions. Him being my defense means that he protects me when I can't do it myself. Give God permission to fight for you!!!

FINDING BALANCE

a) The law of sowing and reaping.
b) God wants to make you prosper.
c) There is grace in being able to reap the harvest.

ACTIVATION – Take a special seed/faith offering.

PRINCIPLE: The law of sowing and reaping works.

ASK YOURSELF: Have you been seeing the law work for you?

MEMORY VERSE: 2 Corinthians 9:10 – Now he that ministereth seed to the sower both minister bread for your food and multiply your seed sown, and increase the fruits of your righteousness.

REAL LIFE: A lot of people are collecting money for their "ministry" find the balance of faith and manipulation.

In the year 2020, there was a pandemic that was released in the earth. This caused the majority of churches to close down their physical locations and to have church online. From this arose a lot of people preaching, praying and prophesying. The thing that has also come up is everyone taking an offering. Cashapp, PayPal and Apple Pay, were all made available to sow. Many times the things that were said were not of substance, it was just "churchy" stuff, but people were giving.

This is the thing, there is nothing wrong with sowing. He gives seed to the sower, for you to sow and plant, as well seed that will be ground to make bread. Not only that but He wants to multiply the seed, that he gave you, and the stuff you have sown. The reason that you sow is not because you are being manipulated into anything but because you believe that His word says that he will give you seed. If you got $5, he gave you seed to sow, or buy something to eat, but He will multiply the seed that has been sown.

Your job is to sow in faith. This is how you can tell if you are being manipulated into giving. When they promise you that if you sow that you're going to get something. We cannot manipulate God into doing something by giving. What we can do is sow in faith, that God is going to move for us. Just as we can not manipulate God, don't allow man, under the ruse of prophetic ministry to manipulate you. Give because you have purposed it in your heart. Give because you want to. Sow because you are cheerful at it, not because you have been tricked into a Ponzi scheme of prophetic ministry.

GOOD STEWARD

a) He gives seed to the sower, but he also shows you how to maintain.
b) Stewardship takes practice.
c) Finding balance in substance.

ACTIVATION – Figure out how to make a budget!

PRINCIPLE: God does not want you to be a shooting star, he wants you to stay and shine.

ASK YOURSELF: Am I willing to be educated, to gain stability in my finances?

MEMORY VERSE: Matthew 25:29 – For unto everyone that hath shall be given, and he shall have abundance: but from him that hath not shall be taken away even that which he hath.

REAL LIFE: Your little bit can be multiplied, if you're not lazy, waiting for it to happen.

It is God's plan to make sure that we are provided for. He would that we would prosper and be in health as our souls prosper. He is a rewarder of those that are seeking him diligently. Can we accept that? Can you accept the fact that God has called us to prosper in live in great grace? Now, that you have done that, I need you to make sure that you can maintain it. The story in Matthew talks about a CEO who gives money to some of his managers. The CEO comes back after so many days and the managers come back after multiplying their money, except one person. That one manager showed up and said I know you, so I just brought your money back.

The interesting part about this story is the response of the CEO. He called him lazy, because he didn't multiply or increase the income that he was given. He even told him that he could have put it in the bank so that it can at least gain interest. We have to catch the revelation that God has put into this parable. That parable is specific in his laziness and his inability to cause increase to the thing that he was given. We are supposed to multiply and increase.

After multiplication and increase we are supposed to be able to be sustained and sustainable. He will make you a lender...how? How is he going to make you a lender if everything you get you spend? God has checks and balances. There is life and death, sun and moon, sick and healing. You've got to figure out the balance so that he can cause increase to your life, give you stability as well as prosper you to prosper the kingdom and others in your community.

SOWING

a) He gives seed to the sower.
b) What does sowing look like?
c) Is there a correct way to sow?

ACTIVATION – Set a goal to give a specific amount to sow, into someone or into a ministry that is building and reaching people.

PRINCIPLE: Sowing is part of a principle, but necessary in order to receive.

ASK YOURSELF: Are you willing to let go of something in order to get?

MEMORY VERSE: Luke 8:5 – A sower went out to sow his seed: and as he sowed, some fell by the wayside; and it was trodden down, and the fowls of the air devoured it.

REAL LIFE: Sowing is investing, and it takes time for it to grow, but you've got to invest.

This is always a big thing to deal with. When many people consider giving or sowing, we are looking at losing something. When you look at sowing, you will realize that it really does mean taking money out of your hand and putting it somewhere, believing that it will grow, can be scary. The text tells a parable about how a sower went out to sow and some fell by the wayside.

A couple of things to look at; the sower went to sow. He purposed in his heart to give. It was something that he went to do, not by accident but his point in going that way was to sow. This is the other thing, he SOWED!!! He went to sow, and he sowed on purpose. He spied out the land, he had already turned it over in order for the seed to be received and he sowed. The rest of that scripture talks about the kind of ground that he sowed into. Some of that ground was stony, some did not take its roots. This is the thing; the bible says that the sower. This was his profession. Do you think he did not look and see that there was stones and things that the seed may fall onto?

We try to make sure that the ground is good, and that's not a bad thing, but sow!!! This is the other thing, it is sometimes difficult to look at your seeds and try and figure out where to sow in order to have the largest harvest. The key thing in all of this is your heart in sowing. Sow!!! Give with the intent that by faith in the word of God that you will reap as you sow, you have got to be able to sow, no matter how much you don't have!!!

BENEVOLENCE

a) It is the job of the church to help the community.
b) The quality of being well meaning – Benevolence
c) Thinking about somebody else is a seed sown.

ACTIVATION – Find someone to bless or a ministry that is helping people.

PRINCIPLE: Doing for others is a part of what we should do as believers.

ASK YOURSELF: Am I concerned about other people as much as I am about me?

MEMORY VERSE: Galatians 6:9 – And let us not be weary in well doing: for in due season we shall reap, if we faint not.

REAL LIFE: People have needs that they do not have the ability to get, it's our job to help.

There is a church in Detroit, that has a food pantry that is trying to feed their community. The church had an evangelism event where they gave away ice cream and BBQ to the community. The evangelism team went out to the neighborhood to gather more people and to pray for people. They didn't know where the church was, but they know exactly where the food pantry was. It had been a stable place for fulfillment for over 20 years. Faithfully, pouring into the lives of people by giving them food, referrals and giving them Jesus.

The book of Acts tells a story about how people did not have any needs at all, because the church made sure that everyone who had needs in the church were able to pour into each other in order to get stable and solid. A couple decided they would only bring a portion of what they had agreed to give and lied and said the bit that they brought was all that they had. They lied, and the bible says that they lied to the Holy Ghost. How did they lie to the Holy Ghost? We don't have a textual reason, we can only assume that the Holy Spirit inspired them to do something, and instead of doing it all the way they lied and ended up dropping dead.

Let me remind you, that It is important to make sure you carry through with what God has told you to do to help someone. I know that he will stretch your faith in giving or in whom to give to. He will call you to give to people you don't want to. He may call you to give beyond yourself. Some people will tell you not to give out of your lack (give when you don't really have enough), but I would rather obey God than man. Be benevolent and give to those in need. Oh, and it's not your job to figure out if they are going to use whatever you give for what you think they should use it for. Trust God to do what He said that he would do, as you do what you will do.

PROPHECY

a) What is prophecy?
b) Why is the prophetic necessary?
c) Who can prophesy?

ACTIVATION – Trust God to speak to you, one word, about each student. Then have the students give one word to you.

PRINCIPLE: God wants to, and does, speak to us all the time.

ASK YOURSELF: Have I been listening to God when He speaks to me?

MEMORY VERSE: 1 Corinthians – 14:31 – For you can all prophesy one by one, that all may learn and all my be encouraged.

REAL LIFE: God is always talking, am I listening to how and when He is speaking to me.

Before understanding the flow of the prophetic we have to be able to enlist the truth of why we do what we do. Why is it important to bring the word of the Lord to the earth? It is the written word of the Lord that lets us know that we are anchored. It is the only thing that is unshakable and infallible. An explanation of the prophetic is necessary. *Prophesy – The mind, will and heart of God migrating and manifesting in words or actions, to the mind, will and heart of man.*

As a believer it is clear in scripture that we should be able to talk to our father and our Father wants to talk back to us. *Luke 11:11-13 says, If a son shall ask bread of any of you that is a father, will he give him a stone? Or if he ask a fish, will he for a fish give him a serpent? (12) Or if he shall ask an egg, will he offer him a scorpion? (13) If ye then, being evil, know how to give good gifts unto your children: how much more shall your heavenly Father give the Holy Spirit to them that ask him?*

If we ask our heavenly Father to speak to us...He will, through his Holy Spirit speak to us. Why do we have these teachings and stories that we have to be "careful" regarding hearing from the Lord? Why do we question if God is still speaking? What kind of father says one thing and nothing else, ever again to his child? Our father wants to speak to us, about anything and everything. If we ask God to speak to us, he will speak to us. The question is do we allow our perceptions and preconceived notions regarding the Lord to be the thing that talks us out of our relationship with God.

1 Corinthians 14:12 – (12) Even so ye, forasmuch as ye are zealous of spiritual gifts, seek that ye may excel to the edifying of the Church. 1 Corinthians 14:3 – (3) But he that prophesies speaketh unto men to edification, exhortation and comfort. As we explore scripture, it is clear that God wants us to build the house as well as cause us to excel in edifying the church. Edification can come through the prophetic. The depth of the prophetic equates to the depth of our experience with God and our commitment to His word. Not the prophetic word, his Logos word. (Shipman, 2014)

Shipman, R. 2014, Let Them Prophesy

THE WRITTEN WORD

a) The importance of the word of God when it comes to the prophetic.
b) Why do we want to prophesy and not know the word?
c) Can you prophesy the written word of God?

ACTIVATION – Prophetic Exercise - Give a scripture to someone in the group to encourage them.

PRINCIPLE: Heaven and earth will disappear, but His word will never be blown over.

ASK YOURSELF: Do I know the personality of God?

MEMORY VERSE: Hebrews 4:12 – For the word of God is quick and powerful, and sharper than any two edged sword, piercing even to the dividing asunder of soul and spirit, and the joints and marrow, and is the discerner of the thoughts and intents of the heart.

REAL LIFE: In order to really understand the voice of God you have to know His Word.

We have to understand that the word of the Lord is our anchor in every area as a believer. Prophetic ppl/Prophets have the ability to see and hear in the spirit realm. It is the word of the Lord that keeps us grounded so that we are not just floating and pulling from the "spirit". Our source is only God. We don't use conjuring or extra stuff to get the word of the Lord...we wait for it.

Isaiah, Jeremiah, Elijah and all the prophets of the Lord, said that the "word of the Lord came to them". We don't have to chase a word; we wait for him to bring it to us. The foundation of the prophetic is 2 things. Prayer and the word of God. We have to understand what He has said before we can understand what He is saying... Many people want to jump into ministry and the prophetic with no foundation. There are some people who have been operating in the prophetic before being able to understand or comprehend the written word of God. That's not unusual, but the rhema word, should ALWAYS coincide with the written word of
God. It is how we measure if God is saying it. You can understand God's personality in His word.

So faith comes, by hearing the prophetic word of the Lord, and hearing the word of the Lord comes from His written word. I also want to be sure that your faith is moved from the same place it has been for the last 10 years and blast you forward. If the word of Lord looks and sounds the same to you as it has 10 years ago, there has been no growth. The word of God is living, so it's always growing and moving forward and showing different sides. Let the word of God be your anchor in all things!

MEDIA (TV, RADIO & MUSIC)

a) Has God ever spoken to you though a television show?
b) Can God use secular artist and music?
c) What are some ways God uses media?

ACTIVATION – Prophetic Exercise – Ask God for a secular song or TV show that speaks to someone in the room.

PRINCIPLE: God's voice is not regulated to the church or formal ministry.

ASK YOURSELF: Do I know when God is speaking to me through other avenues than what I am used to?

MEMORY VERSE: Hebrews 4:12 – For the word of God is quick and powerful, and sharper than any two-edged sword, piercing even to the dividing asunder of soul and spirit, and the joints and marrow, and is the discerner of the thoughts and intents of the heart.

REAL LIFE: Sometimes that emotional response that we get from music, tv and music may not be about emotionalism it could be God speaking to you.

God speaks to us in several different ways and through several different things. So one of the ways God will speak to us is through media. That is TV, Radio, movies and the like. I enjoy television and movies. Yes, the prophet is carnal. And my favorite show of all time is Friends. I remember one time the characters Ross and Rachel had broken up, and they were trying to figure out how to get back together. Rachel wrote Ross a 16-page letter...front and back (lol) and they agreed to get back together.

The problem was Ross feel asleep reading it, so when Rachel asked him if he agreed, He just agreed because he wanted to be with her. I was cracking up, until God said you do that. I looked around that great room and asked, who are you talking to? He clearly said, you agree to things without considering the cost or what you've just admitted to committing to so you can get what you think you want/need. I responded Lord, this is Friends...not us. And his response was...did I not call you my friend and not my servant. Know what you have agreed to in serving me, your life is not your own.

God speaks to us and can speak to us through whatever avenue we are listening from. So, if He can get your attention through a song, a rap, a movie or a television show, He will, because you matter that much to Him.

JOURNALING

a) How do you know when God is speaking to you?
b) Journaling has always been about writing how I feel, how do I hear God with it?
c) What questions can I NOT ask God?

ACTIVATION – Prophetic Exercise – Ask God a question and write down the answer He gives you.

PRINCIPLE: Write it down...don't just try to remember it...record it!!!

ASK YOURSELF: Do you remember all of what God speaks to you?

MEMORY VERSE: Hebrews 4:12 – For the word of God is quick and powerful, and sharper than any two-edged sword, piercing even to the dividing asunder of soul and spirit, and the joints and marrow, and is the discerner of the thoughts and intents of the heart.

REAL LIFE: Write it so you won't forget it. Write it so you can rehearse it. Write it so you'll always have it.

Journaling is basically writing down the conversation that you have with God. Not just what you say but what He says back to you as well. Just like any other relationship, in order for it to develop and to increase in intimacy, you've got to open up and talk about some things. It is necessary for you to discuss how you feel and why you feel what you feel. If you never ask the right questions you will never get the right answers.

While journaling can be eye opening, it can also be jarring as well. When you discover the "person" you have been hearing all of this time has been filtered through your own heart and feelings towards those that have abused you in authority is...wow!!!

Every time I do a training and teaching on journaling, I always get that one person that only hears correction from God. If this is the case for you, I would really evaluate your relationship...not with God, but with your parents, specifically your father. If every time your father talked to you, he was yelling at you, that relationship would not be productive, and conversations wouldn't really be growth inspiring. This kind of relationship will instill bitterness and probably a bit of rebellion. This would be why you always hear God correcting you.

We filter most of what we sense and feel from God through our previous relationships with people in authority and mainly our parents. This does not mean that every time you hear from God it will be something lovely and filled with butterfly kisses. What it means, is that every time He speaks to you, if its correction, redirection or whatever it is, it will always be loving and to protect you, like the loving father He is.

DISCERNING OF SPIRITS

a) What is the difference between discernment and discerning of spirits?
b) What do I do when I "discern a spirit"?
c) Can this gift be corrupted?

ACTIVATION – Your last emotional blow up or outburst, when was it, what spirit was behind it?

PRINCIPLE: Sometimes it's the who not the what is happening.

ASK YOURSELF: What spiritual motivation is happening behind all of the stuff happening in my life.

MEMORY VERSE: Hebrews 4:12 – For the word of God is quick and powerful, and sharper than any two-edged sword, piercing even to the dividing asunder of soul and spirit, and the joints and marrow, and is the discerner of the thoughts and intents of the heart.

REAL LIFE: Write it so you won't forget it. Write it so you can rehearse it. Write it so you'll always have it.

It is easy for people to assume that discernment and discerning of spirits are the same. They are similar but not the same. Discernment is the ability to tell right from wrong. It's when you walk into a room and you feel like there is something wrong, you can "discern" that something is not right or that something is wrong. Discerning of spirits, lets you know the who behind what is happening and doesn't focus on the what.

The gift of discerning of spirits is not regulated to church and ministry. Based on the scripture of 1 Corinthians 12:10, we see it grouped with the other prophetic gifts. Does this mean that the gift of discerning of spirits is regulated to prophetic ministry and realizing if the source of that prophetic word is given by God or not? Sort of, but it's not regulated to what we believe is prophetic ministry today. We should see and hear the word of the Lord spoken over our children, within our marriages, in our churches, jobs and at the gas station, and we would be able to discern what and who the source is.

Not only that, but where words come from anybody's mouth, the person who operates in the gift of discerning of sprits, will be able to know what the source is, bitterness, God, grace, trauma etc. The best part is that this gift is given by the Holy Spirit, if he is in you, guess what, You can operate freely in this gift. The Holy Spirit distributes to us all freely, the way to grow in this gift is to use it.

TONGUES AND INTERPRETATION

a) Tongues = language
b) Interpretation = what is meant by what is said and the intent
c) How does God use any of this???

ACTIVATION – Pray and Ask God for the interpretation of a "Language"

PRINCIPLE: Languages are given for communication, God gifted us to understand.

ASK YOURSELF: Have I taken the time to understand and listen?

MEMORY VERSE: James 3:5 – In the same way the tongue is a small part of the body, but it can brag about doing important things. A large forest can be set on fire by a little flame.

REAL LIFE: There are things, you won't understand in and auditory way, but you will in your heart, intent.

The holiday season is upon us and many are planning on getting things done and purchasing gifts for their friends and family. Have you ever gone to a family event or with friends and people start doing "shop talk"? You know, the people in the medical field start talking about that stuff and then the people in ministry are talking about church stuff. You're not really associated with either and you're just sitting there looking and nodding.

Here is the thing. Many times we sit and recognize that the gift of tongues and interpretation was designated to the use of and earthly or heavenly language. I want to take it a little further and push you into understanding that sometimes it's more than that. There is a jargon, or "a language" that is spoken in different arenas. There is a silent language for the person who comes into a gather with people of the opposite race, and you see that one person of the same race as you, that conversation that is had is loud and clear between you two.

There is a language that is had between the wealthy and the desperate. There is a language for the broken and the bruised. You may hear one thing but the person who has been anointed to operate in the gift of interpretation can hear beyond what is being verbally said and interpret the language in order to build the kingdom as well as to support the individual. Tongues are a sign for unbelievers. Imagine walking into a meeting at Apple, and you not knowing much about computers are able to communicate their designs to others. It puts you in a position to reach people that you normally wouldn't. You're looking to hear French and interpret that. Some have had an experience of interpreting their prayer language. Go further, stretch your faith and interpret the language of the lost and broken as a sign to them that Jesus loves them!!!

GIFTS OF HEALING

a)   What is the gift of healing and who can possess it?
b)   Is there anything special needed to work in this gift?
c)   Why is this gift not used like the rest?

ACTIVATION – Pray for healing!!!

PRINCIPLE: Gifts of healing operate and function under the unction of the Holy Spirit, just like all the others...it operates by your faith.

ASK YOURSELF: Have I allowed healing to flow through me?

MEMORY VERSE: Psalms 107:20 – He sent His word, and healed them, and delivered them from all their destructions.

REAL LIFE: You are the answer to what has made the world around you sick.

This lesson is going to show us the grace that God has given us through His Holy Spirit. The bible says when Christ ascended, He gave gifts to men. There is another place in scripture that gives us an exhaustive list of the gifts of God that are designed to build and pour into the body of Christ. They are to be used in order to bring glory to God and be a testimony of His love and mighty power. This gift seems to be lacking, probably because it is one that has been abused for attention and money making,

I want to show you that healing is supposed to be done on the inside and the outside. The bible says in 3 John, that He would that we would prosper and be in health, as our souls prosper. Some of us are so focused on the healing to happen to the physical body that we have missed that God has also called us to heal the inside. Yes, you!!! If we are living epistles read of men, that means we carry his word. Look at the memory verse again. We have read that several times and seen it different, let's look at it from the healing perspective.

He sent his word and healed them is usually seen as one thing, but it's actually, he sent his word. His word was sent to do something cut, create, form and then he healed them. Well, you are the word that he sent. How does that make any sense? Let's fast forward to Mark 16, where He SENT them to preach and heal the sick of ALL MANNER of diseases. We are so focused on healing the physical that you forgot about the mind and the emotions that also need to be healed. The best part is that you are the answer!!! By faith you operate in all of the gifts. Just as you pray, prophesy, dance and shout. Heal the sick!!!

WORKING OF MIRACLES

a) What goes into seeing a miracle?
b) What is a miracle?
c) Is this a gift like all the other gifts of the spirit?

ACTIVATION – Pray for miracles!!!

PRINCIPLE: The gift of working miracles is usually seen in the patient person.

ASK YOURSELF: Am I willing to put the work in for miracles?

MEMORY VERSE: 1 Corinthians 12:10a – To another the working of miracles; to another prophecy; to another discerning of spirits.

REAL LIFE: A regular job requires 40 hours a week, if you want increase in your finances you have to put more work in...want to see miracles...add more to what you're working.

The Father has released several gifts to the body, for our maturation and development in the world and the kingdom. This is the thing, when we start talking about miracles, we have to ask ourselves, do they still happen, what are they and how can I get one. In this scripture the word miracle means, mighty, power or ability to do. So, a miracle is not just somebody coming back to life, it is literally the ability to do or accomplish something you couldn't do before.

Working in this scripture speaks of the effects of something. So, in order to get a door, open you have to push it. The working in the opening of the door is the push. Something had to be done in order to open the door. God has called us to do things that couldn't be done by somebody else's power. Have you ever been somewhere and people were trying to figure out how to get something done and you just walked over and fixed it, lifted it or answered it? You just worked a miracle.

Here is the big thing, you have to do something about it. Our faith activates it, but the work is not faith, it is something that is done. Faith is something that is unseen, work is something that you can see and that is tangible. If that is warfare, worship, tongues, dancing, shouting until the miracle, by your faith begins to formulate, that's what you do until you see the miracle begin to manifest itself fully. This is why our principle speaks of patience. Working miracles sometimes takes time, it takes work and energy and faith, all of that combined will produce the miracles that we are looking for, now that's a real gift!!!

OPERATING IN LOVE

d) How is operating in love a gift.
e) Is love spiritual?
f) What does "operate in love" look like?

ACTIVATION – Put your gift down and deal with your heart. What do you need to deal with right now?

PRINCIPLE: Operating in the gifts is amazing, but it takes the Holy Spirit to really love, just like operating in the gifts.

ASK YOURSELF: All of the operation I have done, have I been able to do it while loving myself enough to accept what God says about me?

MEMORY VERSE: 1 Corinthians 12:31 – But covet earnestly the best gifts: and yet shew I unto you a more excellent way.

REAL LIFE: Love isn't love until you've given it away.

Commissioned had a song out years ago and a line in the song said: What good, would love do you, if you keep it to yourself? Somebody needs to receive it from you, so give it to somebody else. Love isn't love till you've given it away. Just like every other gift that we have received from the Lord, it is a gift, and the gift is here to be given. From tongues, interpretation, prophesy, miracles, helps, faith and all the other gifts given to us, they should be used and given to people too.

This is the interesting thing about love and those gifts. It's really easy to give them to everyone else and difficult to minister them to ourselves. We can prophesy all day to people and not look in the mirror and prophesy to ourselves. The first area of ministry we have to make sure we deal with is to deal with ourselves. This is why journaling is a great tool of activation for prophetic ministry because you get to hear God for you about you.

This memory verse is the key. It is the key to real operation in the kingdom. It is the real demonstration of the kingdom. This scripture tells us to go hard after the best gifts. The best gifts are the ones that you like. I can't tell you what the best gift is for you, nor can you for me. The next scripture tells us that Paul wanted to show us a more excellent way. The next chapter talks about how love is. But let's look at that part, excellent way. This means to go beyond. So, not just the gifts of ministry, but go beyond that and reach people. Love them like Christ. That goes for you too!!! You are your own worst critic, how about before the end of this year, you figure out how to Love yourself, as much as you love the other gifts...go beyond and love you!!!

Made in the USA
Monee, IL
14 January 2021